CARDINAL POINTS

CARDINAL POINTS

Poems on St. Louis Cardinals Baseball

by Joseph Stanton

McFarland & Company, Inc., Publishers
Jefferson, North Carolina, and London

Library of Congress Cataloguing-in-Publication Data

Stanton, Joseph, 1949–
    Cardinal points : poems on St. Louis Cardinals baseball / by
Joseph Stanton.
       p.   cm.
    Includes index.
    ISBN 0-7864-1373-5 (softcover : 60# alkaline paper) ∞
    1. St. Louis Cardinals (Baseball team)—Poetry. 2. Baseball
teams—Poetry.   3. Baseball—Poetry. I. Title.
    PS3569.T33365C37   2002
    811'.54—dc21   2002009907

British Library cataloguing data are available

Cover art: *Gashouse Gang* by Robert Thom
(National Baseball Hall of Fame)

Manufactured in the United States of America

McFarland & Company, Inc., Publishers
  Box 611, Jefferson, North Carolina 28640
    www.mcfarlandpub.com

For the Cardinals fans in my family:
my parents, my sister Barbara, her husband Jim,
and their children—Doug, Greg, and Karen.

And for my wife, Barbara, and our children, Susan and David,
in hopes that this book will persuade them
to cultivate an affection for red birds.

Acknowledgments

The author would like to thank the editors of these publications, in which the following poems have appeared, often in different versions: *Aethlon* ("Catcher," "Curt Flood in Center," "Harry Caray's Voice," "Lou Brock Running," and "Stan, the Statue"); *The Cortland Review* ("The Space-Time Continuum and the Slow Eye of Stan the Man"); *Elysian Fields* ("Elysian Curve," "Enos Slaughter Scores from First," "Julian Javier at Second," and "Stealing Home"); *Fan* ("Dick Groat at Short"); *Hapa* ("Stan 'The Man' Musial"); and *New York Quarterly* ("Musial," another version of "Stan 'The Man' Musial"); *Spitball* ("Bob Gibson on the Mound" and "The Utility of Mike Shannon").

"Catcher" is from *Imaginary Museum: Poems on Art* by Joseph Stanton and is reprinted by permission of Time Being Books, copyright ©1999 by Time Being Press, all rights reserved.

"Stealing Home" was reprinted in *Line Drives: 100 Contemporary Baseball Poems*, an anthology published by Southern Illinois University Press.

All photographs and the cover painting, *The Gashouse Gang* by Robert Thom, were provided by the National Baseball Hall of Fame Library, Cooperstown, New York, and are reproduced by permission.

Contents

THE 1940S AND 50S

THE 1960S AND 70S

THE 1980S AND 90S

THE 2000s

POSTGAME POINTS

Preface: Cardinal Land

Cardinal Land is a vast, mysterious field of play. It is clear that its home plate resides in a medium-sized city at the intersection of the Mississippi and Missouri rivers known as St. Louis, but the dimensions of that field are shifting and incalculable.

My poems touch upon over a hundred years of Cardinals baseball, but there has been no effort to represent all the Redbird eras equally. The 1964 team is, for instance, more fully covered because it is a team that fascinated me in my youth.

It will be evident in what follows that I am a partisan, a fanatic for the St. Louis Cardinals. Other poets will have to speak up for all the other great teams. Baseball fandom has many countries.

PROLOGUE

Cardinal

Cardinal is, above all else, a red letter word:
a strikingly hued approbation as much as a bird;
a matter of foremost importance, paramount;

a lofty rank from which popes spring eternal.
Rules, sins, directions, and numbers count
as cardinal, if they are worth the trouble.

Cardinal red blushes dark, vivid, and deep.
Cardinalis cardinalis is a species name that bears
repeating—a sudden trill of lilting, swelling

long-song—limpid, floating beyond glorious,
across summer afternoons arising from a finch,
     North American and male, hopping from branch

to branch or perched on two sides of a bat
or rounding third and heading for a home
that seems so very far away, at least

two plane rides and several decades of grief,
against all probability but compelled
by desire, a matter of foremost importance.

Cardinal also means "hinge upon" and
"belong to"; and—year after year,
in sickness or in post-season—I do.

Opening Game, 1899

More than a hundred Aprils
ago a re-used, brand-new team came to town.

In Cleveland they had been Spiders,
but in St. Louis scarlet outfits
revealed, for the first time, their true color
and they were reborn as Cardinals.

Their ace, a certain Denton "Cy" Young,
won that first game handily, ten to one:
helped by the play of O'Conner and Tabeau.

At the old century's dark end, a bright
red tradition had begun to glow.

THE 1920S AND 30S

Branch Rickey Invents Thirty Years of Winning

Above all it was Rickey's clever schemes
that raised the Cards, despite poverty,
to be among the greatest of all teams.

His Knothole Gang tinted
an entire city Redbird red
and browned out the other team.

His spring trainings
in warmer weathers
made his teams readier.

The 20s was a time much like our own.
New York teams were buying the best guys
and buying, thereby, winning seasons.

But Rickey devised, against this grain,
a system of farming that harvested
NL flags again and again

in the 20s,
the 30s,
and the 40s.

His players hated his mean, skinflint ways,
and all that he did to feather his own nest,
but none denied he was the cleverest.

Grover Cleveland Alexander Faces Tony Lazzeri in the Seventh Inning of the Seventh Game of the 1926 World Series

"He could have done it in his sleep."
The old expression claims an ease
that no one ever has
who tries to do hard things well,

but Alex was asleep when Hornsby called.
He'd won the day before and had
gone out to sip "a few" with friends
and never really got to bed.

His painstakingly slow walk from
bullpen to mound is the stuff of legend.
Did he stop to pick daisies? Did he
zigzag to chat with every fielder?

Alex claims he had one eye
on Lazzeri all the way, knowing
the rookie slugger was anxious
beyond belief, pawing and clawing,

hopping in and out of the box,
hoping to be the year's hero,
an almost-great Casey at the plate.
Then suddenly Alex was all there,

tossing three quick warm-ups,
and ready, very ready to go,
set to be the deft, uncanny
pitching machine he had been

all down the stretch. His little hat
cocked, slightly askew as always,
he leaned in, knowing he would try
to make Lazzeri go for bad balls.

The key would be a high, tight toss
that Tony could smack far and foul.

Remembering it in the 70s,
Les Bell tells the tale:

"For fifty years that ball has been traveling.
It has been foul anywhere from an inch
to twenty feet.... But I was standing
on third base, and I'll tell you—
it was foul all the way. All the way."

After that, "the old man" had Tony in hand,
fast as a flask in a hip pocket.

The last swinging strike
came on an outside curve
Lazzeri would've needed
a subway ride to reach.

Grover Cleveland Alexander

Rogers Hornsby on His One-Punch Knockout of an Opposing Manager

I couldn't
make any headway
against him

talking.

Rogers Hornsby

The Incomparable Rogers Hornsby

This level of perfection has its quirks,
and teammates scoffed at his proscriptions,
his refusal to watch a film or read a book
for fear his batting eye might lose precision.

But who could argue with results this fine?
His average was .358 lifetime,
and then there was 1924,
the year he hit .424 and led
the league in slugging and walks received.

With careful tending of his precious eye,
he reached base at least half the times he tried.

Sunny Jim Bottomley's Big Day

In 1924 when Hornsby batted .424
the man who hit behind him
had some days to grin about, too.

In mid September,
Sunny Jim—a laughing, jocose kind of guy,
his hat always cocked

rakishly over his left eye—
had a day that fans remembered
long after they'd forgotten

the Cards' dismal finish that year,
Rickey's last as manager.
Bottomley's six hits and twelve RBIs

in six at bats—three singles, one double,
and two homeruns (one a grandslam)
set a record that outlived him,

made his hitting style almost as renowned
as that other infamous thing about him,
his solar-powered smile.

The Night They Kidnapped Flint Rhem

In the heat of the race in 1930
star Cardinal pitcher Flint Rhem,
well known for his problems with the bottle,
disappeared for two days and two nights.

When he resurfaced, smelling of liquor,
he explained his absence to his manager,
weaving a tale of high intrigue,
"Some great big guys snatched me
and blindfolded me and locked me up
in a room in some stinking old hotel.
They held a gun to my head and forced me
to keep drinking whiskey until I passed out."

When Gabby Street expressed some doubts
and threatened fines, Rhem remonstrated,
"But they wouldn't take no for an answer, Boss.
It was terrible!" Gabby was, for once, speechless.
Flint's heroically silly little lie
was such a remarkable alibi.

Catcher of the Fastest (Vertical) Fastball

Before he became known as "the Sarge,"
the talkative honcho of the Cards,
Charles "Gabby" Street was a good-field, no-hit
catcher for the Senators of Washington.

There he caught lots of bullets from the gun
of the fastest of them all in those days,
the amazing Walter "Big Train" Johnson.
But the fastest fast one he ever snagged

fell straight down 550 feet
to where he waited unwisely
on the sunbaked, reporter-crowded mall,
below Washington's knife-bright monument,

scanning the sky for what was gently tossed off top
but was screaming down at hundreds of miles
per hour by the time it reach him.
It must have been hard to discern amidst

the fierce August shine of sun and stone;
and no one quite caught the physics of the thing—
that this pitch could have struck him dead.
Gabby was, the papers said, "considerably

jarred by the impact of the ball in his glove."
But it did not keep him from ending the day
backstopping Big Train's 3–1 taming
of Tyrus Cobb's Tigers of Detroit.

Burleigh Grimes:
Wielder of the Last Legal Spitter

Batters found his wet ones uncanny.
They felt at sea or underwater
as they watched his waves break
bizarrely against jagged rocks of sky.

"Old Stubblebeard" was the name they gave him
because he never shaved before the games
he pitched. He'd found the resin he chewed
to juice his spit would sting a shaven face.

His coarse and scowling visage made him seem
an agent of danger, a one-man feud.
John Kiernan wrote that Grimes "looked like a guy
about to commit assault and battery."

And Grimes was armed with iron, pitching
through appendicitis till the end of 31,
beating the Athletics in the last game
of the World Series, with help from Hallahan,

before being rushed to Emergency.
Grimey Grimes, the tough guy's tough guy,
would never have accepted the relief,
but the doc said: operate now or die.

Pepper Martin at bat in the 1931 World Series

The Pepper Martin World Series

In 1931, when America
was depressed in more ways than one,
"the Wild Horse of the Osage,"
"nature's nobleman,"
John "Pepper" Martin,
"a chunky, unshaven hobo who ran
the bases like a berserk locomotive,"

almost singlehandedly destroyed the hopes
of George Earnshaw, Lefty Grove,
and the rest of the last
of Philadelphia's great Athletics—

a triumph of a very common man
in days when most buddies could not spare even
the thinnest of dimes; when sorrow reigned, hard,
and pennies from Heaven only fell in song;

when rookies like Pepper were payed so little,
he chose to hop trains from Oklahoma
to spring training camp in Florida
and showed up late because some ornery cops
nabbed him vagrant and tossed him into jail.

He strove harder than all the rest and dove
head-first to catch the ball or steal the base.
Some complained he made easy plays look hard,
but none could deny the startling grandeur
of Pepper at play in the fall of 31.

Fans who were just as dirt-poor as Pepper
loved to tell the tale of Martin's post-game
chat with the lord high Commissioner
in which Landis declared, "Young man,
I'd like to trade places with you,"
and Pepper replied, "Why, that'll be fine,
Judge, if we can swap salaries, too."

Robert Thom's The Gashouse Gang

At bottom this truncated triangle
has Pepper Martin bursting with desire,
diving headfirst, reaching at an odd angle,
ferociously desperate to get there,
in front of the umpire and under the glove
without regard for safety of head or hands,
embracing the bag with a desperate love,
amid the screaming (unheard here) of the fans,
redecorating his white uniform with the dirt
his slide raises and sprays far and wide.

Often he played injured, discounting any hurt,
sprinting wildly, arms pumping side to side.
He'd come a long way to wear his number one,
and every inch of it had been on the run.

Pepper Martin, Gangster

Before spring training in 34
Pepper pulled up to a small hotel,
and sauntered in, shotgun in hand,
and signed the registry
"Pretty Boy Floyd."

Later, when the town's sheriff steamed in,
backed by every armed man in the county,
Pepper laughed and laughed,
repeatedly berating the posse
for not finding the whole thing funny.

The Greatness of Dizzy Dean

A sharecropper's son,
a genuine barefoot boy,
he beat a college team
when he was only twelve.
A natural in more ways than one
he invented himself
as genuine concoction,
the best
there ever was.

When he finally stuck
in the Bigs,
he won and won and won
until a line drive
broke his toe
and the magic
of his arm
came
undone.

In his golden days
he would sometimes
win a game
with only fastballs
just to show
he could,
but his curve,
the batters knew,
had that ineluctable twang, too.

The bardic yawp
of his clownish brag
made some forget
his lore
was, indeed, legend.
Forged in the high place
he hurled forth
his undeniably true
tall tales.

Somewhere in the sky, still,
"Me an' Paul" are singing
them pitches in,
one goddam strike after another.
Even that other
shoeless country boy,
facing the heavenly Deans,
is wishing the Elysian Fields
were only Iowa.

Dizzy Dean, Talkin'

Diz loved to socialize and often appeared,
unwanted guest, in the other team's dugout,
one time telling each Dodger exactly how
he was planning to pitch him—daring them
to profit from what proved to be
an accurate, self-inflicted, scouting report—
and then went and shut them out.

A reporter asked what Dean thought of his chances
against the American League All-Stars.
"Them guys? I could go on bread and water
all week and beat them," was his reply.
His boasts he thought the most common of sense:
"If you say you're gonna do somethin'
and you do it, then it ain't braggin'."

More spectacular than Yogi Berra in his
abuse of the English language, old Diz
really said all the things he said.
"Don't fail to miss tomorrow's game."
"He slud into third."
They "returned to their respectable bases."
"He's standing confidentially at the plate."

When Diz caught a ball with his head, newsprint
blossomed a field day of quotable quips.
"X Rays of Dean's Head Show Nothing,"
declared the famous headline. When asked
about his brother's recovery from the injury,
Paul Dean told reporters: "Diz wasn't hurt bad.
All he was doing was talkin', just talkin'."
When asked what Diz had said, Paul explained,
"He wasn't sayin' anything. He was just talkin'."

Ducky in Detroit

For average and for power Ducky was
among the greatest. A bad ball hitter
in more ways than one and quick with his fists
with anyone who gave him lip (even Leo).

Medwick they all say was the meanest man.

He slid with spikes high to knock Marv Owens
off the bag at third in the seventh game
of the Series against Detroit in 34
when the Cards already had a huge lead.

Frustrated Tiger fans outraged beyond
imagining, soon began to shower
Joe in left with their disaffection—
a cornucopia of fruits (apples,
oranges, bananas, a watermelon
or two), wadded programs and newspapers,
a dangerous array of bottles.

Paul Gallico described the bizarre scene:
"Every face in the crowd, women and men,
was distorted with rage. Mouths were torn wide,
open eyes glistened and shone in the sun.
All fists were clenched." And then
Landis ordered Ducky out of the game.

A beanball toward the end of his career
hospitalized him for days and, some say,
softened his brutality, and he became,
in later years, the tenderest of coaches,
teaching young men how to murder
the ball.

Ducky's Visit to the Vatican

Hello, Your Holiness,
I'm Joseph Medwick.
I, too, used to be
a Cardinal.

Joe Medwick

THE 1940s AND 50s

America's Team

The KMOX broadcasts beamed way out West.
The Cards' mouth also shouted way down South
and on and on even into Mexico.
All the Midwest listened and some Canadians.

Although not bolstered by New York money
and perhaps because of that very fact,
the Cards became, in the Radio Age,
America's team, even beyond the US of A.

Mort Cooper's Numbers Game

Mort Cooper, the Cards' ace in 42,
feared that the unlucky thirteen
on his back might turn out to be
the stopping point for his victories

so when he'd finally won thirteen
he decided he needed a change of jersey
and wore Mancuso's fourteen to win the next
and his brother's fifteen for the fifteenth.

It must have been a sight to see him pitch
his next game squeezed into little Ken O'Dea's
number sixteen, but he won that one, too,
claiming constriction helped him concentrate.

He kept on winning, mostly, in all shirts,
baggy or tight, long or short, until the Cards
had won the pennant and Mort had achieved
the MVP and his twenty-second victory.

The Cooper Brothers

In the 40s the Cards had
two super Coopers—
one to pitch,
one to catch.

Every strike that Mort hove
and Walker caught
was a kind of family conversation,
an act, so to speak, of brotherly love.

Mort was loud, reckless, ruddy, joking;
Walker quiet, careful, blond, unsmiling;
and they loved each other dearly.

What one would give the other would take,
doing their best down the stretch
or in the Series
when most was at stake.

Pass the Biscuits, Mirandy

The Cards' theme song in 42
was "Pass the Biscuits, Mirandy"—

a goofy, Spike Jones tune
about a murderous mountaineer
and his wife's deadly pastry.

It kept the Cards loose and laughing
all through what Eddie Epstein deems

"the most significant
stretch drive
in major league history."

Edward Hopper's *Nighthawks* Consider the 1942 World Series

"I'm rooting for the Cardinals anyway,"
she mutters staring at her pack of matches.

"No way the Yanks can lose!" he declares
to his wife, the counterman, and the world

in general. "They creamed that Mort Cooper,
and he's the only real pitcher they've got.

This guy Beazley they're putting on the mound
tomorrow? A punk kid. I'll bet the Yankees

chew him up and spit him out in the first.
No way this thing is going more than five."

Edward Laning's *Saturday Afternoon at Sportsman's Park, 1944*

Somewhere out there there was a war,
but Roosevelt had let the games

go on, and by some miracle
the Browns beat out the Yanks and fans

in St. Louis had the Series
all to themselves and Sportsman Park

became a cacophonous town meeting.
Laning's painting captures the scene,
rendering the fans gigantic,
the players tiny and demeaned.

Musial, Mize, and DiMaggio in Moiliili

During World War II
major league stars
battled in the Pacific theatre
of Honolulu Stadium
for inter-service bragging rights—
the Army may have had "Joltin'" Joe,
but the Navy had his brother Dom
and guys like Stan "The Man"
and "The Big Cat," Johnny Mize.

Even the little town
where I live now
was, in those days,
a major league metropolis—
the redoubtable Aiea Hilltoppers
sported pro stars.

It's hard to hold in mind,
but good to know, that—
were I seated in my Honda Accord,
parked in a certain spot
on Isenberg Street
on a certain day in June of 1944—
a prodigious home run
by the great Joe DiMaggio
would have blasted through my window.

Harry "The Cat" Brecheen
in the 1946 World Series

For an Oklahoma boy, like Brecheen,
growing up in the 20s and 30s,
the Cards were the only team to dream on.
This was one feline in love with birds.
(In later years he became an Oriole.)
They called Harry "The Cat"
because of his prance and pounce.

Catching every ball hit his way
kept his ERA falling from year to year,
but the nickname fit his pitching, too:
the sneaky speed, the startling curve,
and then there was that infamous screwball.
He'd studied the Red Sox hitters
all during spring training,

and he was always clever, a cool cat
who loved autumnal temperatures.
He toyed with the Red Sox in 46—
fast and slow, in and out, high and low—
bending the curve against the screw
or reversing that in whichever way
he somehow knew the Sox could not construe.

Enos Slaughter Scores from First to Win the 1946 World Series

Slaughter's desire for home
stopped time in Pesky's
cocked arm.

Clyde Singer's Minor League, 1946

The terrible war is over and yet
in the lingering of this late afternoon
the hard desires at the heart of this action

seem to face a subtle, inexplicable gloom.
The batter, the catcher, and the umpire
await intently in the lurid light

a pitch that we will never see arrive,
while just behind this archetypal tableau
a coach and the next batter intently confer.

These five figures are sculpted by a gleam
severely slanting in from center field,
casting brutal shadows that whisper

this is the end of this, the final chance.
Though the sun must be a bewildering dazzle,
a cruel halo behind the pitcher's head,

the batter holds his bat steady and seems
unconcerned, confident, at the ready, fixed.
Despite the strikes against him, the batter

knows he holds in his hands this moment's axis.
He is the compass wheel. In his poised bat
all the futures crouch baring their fangs.

Stan "The Man" Musial

He made it look easy
so we tried twisting
our little-leagued bodies

into the incipient
violence of his pose,
a spring pulled tight,

crouching deep in the box.
But we could not invoke
the swift accurate stroke

that sent the balls
where they needed to go.
All pitchers feared him,

this gentle, soft-spoken,
line-drive-making machine
who shaped himself

into a question
they could not resolve
no matter how sharp their answers.

There was no hurled prayer
this smiling, chewing oracle
could not fend off.

Preacher Roe on How to Get Musial Out

I throw
four wide ones,
and then
I try to pick him off first.

Stan Musial

The Space-Time Continuum
and the Slow Eye of Stan "The Man"

"Well, you wait for a strike. Then you knock the shit out of it."
—Stan Musial's advice to Curt Flood on hitting

The greatest of hitters, legend has it,
have learned the trick of the slow eye:
a magic that contrives to see in slowed

emotion every turn and twist of hurled
white sphere that rotates its seams
in heightened view for those who've found the way

to note the ball's in-flight curve or swerve
or straight and narrowed path, heart-to-heart,
so that the bat can be administered

precisely dead-on through the line of fire,
for the sake of the sweetest intersection
that sends the pill back the other way,

remaking its career, and the pitcher's, too.
It's as if history were rewriting itself
on the way to the plate; as if the ball

destined for a soft home, a shelter,
a tender pocket of comfort and desire,
were snatched of a sudden by death's

harvesting swing, which must be seen though,
in this case at least, as just another life
arising in what some eyes have come to know.

Whitey Kurowski's Arm

George "Whitey" Kurowski
remarkably excelled
despite a disability.
His deformed right arm had,
they said, more gristle than bone
below the elbow.
But somehow he made

the strange machine
that was his body
into a winning thing.
His shortened limb
became the key
to his teaching himself to be
a vicious pull hitter,

who fiercely crowded the plate,
and everyone marveled
at his play at third,
especially the way
he could rocket that ball
across the field
with his muscular little wing.

Pain in that arm forced him
to retire young,
but throughout the forties
he was one of the best guys
on one of the best teams,
his grasp always exceeding
his reach.

Wally Moon Rising

As a small child in the 1950s
I grieved for the Cardinal's dark days,
so often losing games they should have won.
In that darkness I welcomed the rising
of Wally Moon, whose heavenly promise—
despite his earthbound single eyebrow—
seemed, astrologically, to augur
that even the sky might not be the limit.

But those sad birds never reached the ether.
Our stars were no help at all, and our Moon,
inexplicably, set all too soon.

Red Schoendienst Coming Back

Red Schoendienst lost
one of his lungs to TB

but managed, miraculously,
to come back, showing that,

even with half as much air,
he still had twice the heart.

Arriving at Busch Stadium, Circa 1959

The Busch Stadium of my youth
had lost its sturdy old moniker,
Sportsman's Park,
but no one seemed to mind
in a city still proud to be
first in booze, if not in shoes;
and glad, mostly, to be free
of the Brownies' strangle hold
on last in the American League.

And no one seemed to mind that those
who drove had to stow their Chevys
in all those little roped off lawns,
of folks who lived around the park—
a field of dreams become a way
to make ends meet through a home stand's
many fists full of tax-free fivers.

And no one seemed to mind
that, once cars were stashed
in worn-down patches of brown grass,
there'd be the long, long promenade,
weaving the bright hubbub of streets
awash in game-night mysteries—
a trek toward slow arrivals
of popcorn-scented, organ-toned,
crowd-cacophonied breezy hints,
signs and portents, portents and signs,
subtle electricities of air.

And no one seemed to mind
that our game-intent strollings
were just antic, performing parades
for all the folks sitting on porches,
every porch radio crackling
whatever lovely silliness
our Harry Caray had to say.

Batting Practice at Busch

So many summer days and nights my father would bring me to Busch long before the game was set to start. We would station ourselves in our favorite bleacher spot, dead center in left, in hopes of being in the heart of where the homers land. I always suspected Dad savored early parking more than hopes of homers.

From time to time he'd recount how he'd managed to bare-hand a home run on the fly in the 40s. But that was long ago in a time I thought to be mythological. I wanted only this completely present moment of 1959 with my well-oiled Ken Boyer glove in hand and both my anxious eyes on batting-practice cracks of bats.

It amazed me that the players seemed to care so little for the precious white spheres that would have meant so much to me could I have contrived some way to make them mine. They kicked and tossed the balls around as if they were just warm-up tools, and, of course, that's all they really were, but in my mind they seemed to be round pieces of something somehow wholly beyond the ordinary—sacred relics of a holy here-and-now. When, suddenly, the actual Kenny Boyer suddenly whacked an actual ball high into the still underfilled left-center-field seats, I and several dozen other clowns scrambled, stumbling vaguely toward that general direction, only to see the ball rise high in someone's hand long before we neared the place.

My mother thought I was crazy to care so much for what could be bought in any Sears or Penneys. She came with us once per season, on Ladies' Night, just to see us in our native male habitat. One night she observed with gathering alarm as I cavorted south and north of where she watched me, but then a batting practice ball began its bounce above and to our left and as I ran that way the ball scooted back the other, right in front of Mom who snatched it up and said, "Now, you have one. Let's just relax and watch the game."

It was the only ball I ever got.

John Falter's Saturday Evening Post Cover (May 1, 1954), Showing Stan Musial Signing Autographs for Kids

One of those kids might have been me. At any home game we could count on him. If we waited beneath the ramp where the players had to pass, autographs would come to some of us for as long as the guys were willing to stop and sign. Almost always it was Musial and the rookies who lingered longest. The rookies loved to be asked, though we seldom really knew who they were. Often we were still not sure after long scrutiny of their hurried scrawls. Their names were sometimes not even listed in the infrequently updated rosters we had in hand. Sometimes they were long gone back to one of the bush leagues by the next week.

But Musial was something else. Even his signature was classic and classy with those big rounded loops that lent drama to his calligraphic swings of the pen. Looking back, his patience defies belief, his kindly leanings to the clamorous beseechings from which most of the other stars quickly fled. Game after game that was the way it was on the ramp: the Man and the Kids. It seemed too Norman Rockwell to be true, but it was.

And down through the years my collection of Musial signatures grew, even after he retired. It seemed every year or two we ran into him somewhere—at the shopping mall where my mother worked, at a Hawks game, in Forest Park, at every sort of St. Louis place. When he saw you recognized him, he flashed that wide friendly smile, and, if you asked, he would sign almost anything. Most of mine were on things like soiled scorecards, popcorn megaphones, napkins, paper bags. I never seemed to have a decent piece of paper when we ran into him.

All those kindly signings are gone now, perhaps lost in a flooded basement or the sale of my parents' house. I'm not sure where they went or when or why, but I can never forget Stan the Man's lightning smile, a signifying gesture that said he never took himself too seriously but understood why we kids would never stop pursuing him.

Stan, the Statue:
On the Monument at the Stadium

It looks nothing like him
and makes nothing of its
artistic license beyond
a lurid failure
to resemble.

We want to say The Man
deserves better than this.
But maybe the tribute
fits the subject
in an odd sort of way.

The sculptor could no more
figure out The Man than
could two decades of pitchers.

The inscrutably perfect,
impossible stance
blasts, once again,
a screaming line drive.
No manner of Art
can breeze one past him.

THE 1960S AND 70S

Harry Caray's Voice

His voice rising garish, garrulous
above our barbecue pits was summer.
His deep voice high pitched
to a blue-sky falsetto
when the game was on the line.

Those excited moments stick
to the mind beyond memory of what
happened and why it mattered,
if it did. The excitement
was a game unto itself.

Hearing his voice on my way
to somebody's backyard
or while rounding
some corner on my bike—
I could not know whether

Boyer had slammed a homer,
Musial had laced a timely
line drive, Gibson had drilled
a hole in McCarver's glove
for a third strike on Clemente,

Banks, or Matthews. It was not
the hearing that was so wonderful,
but the overhearing. That voice—
its rise and fall, the chatty
silliness of its commentary,

the outrageous confidence
of its insane predictions
(that so strangely often came true)—
that outrageous, unlovely voice
so wonderful to overhear

from a distance while rounding
a corner on a bike—that voice
meant summer was still out there
like a big, slow Curt Simmons curve
that might never stop floating.

Bill White on First

Injuries shortened White's career,
and kept him shy of halls of fame,
but he was best on first throughout
the years I was a child and his

rich voice and astute laconic
one-liners, the many times Harry
Caray picked him for post-game chat,
defined for me what smart could be.

His smooth, aloof replies hinted
there could be more to life than bats
and balls, and I loved the way
he toyed with Harry's oddest queries,

his voice a kind of smile.

Julian Javier at Second

So many times running
so far from home
so fast
those long legs loping
leaping somehow
perfectly timing
his reach high
into the alien
blue
reaching for
a rounded piece of
sky
almost lost
overhead
just ahead
high in the air
alive with fierce
foreign
cries
he could not quite grasp
yet
leaping anyway
he catches
somehow
the uncatchable
fly

Dick Groat at Short

What would you do with that cleverness
in your hands after all those winning
years wearing Pittsburgh's snazzy black and gold,
after all those years of honing the skill
of banging the ball where the holes were?

What would you do if you had one bad year
and the black-sleeved team you loved
decided you were through and traded you
for next to nothing and you found yourself
wearing the red sleeves of the enemy?

What would you say to your weathered face
in the unforgiving mirror regarding
the merciless shine of your balding head,
best and worst reminder of all
that would never come back again?

What would be your best revenge but to play
better than ever, doing everything
smarter, smoother; lifting weights all winter;
running, running down the cold, bitter nights;
chasing shadows of what you thought you'd lost?

Ken and Clete

The Boyer boys were
so alike in appearance,
in excellence of play,
and, by happenstance,
they both found themselves
manning the hot corner.

Though both were raised uprightly
in a close-knit family
of ardent Cardinals devotees,
regretfully,
one brother ended up
only
a New York Yankee.

Ken Boyer at Third

He moved with such graceful strength—
his glove smooth as a spoon scooping cream—
that fans failed to understand
how hard he was trying to deserve
his dream come true: a country boy,
Ozarks born and bred, raised to worship
the mighty Cardinals, gods riding
the air, crackling in the static
rural radio reception.

Kenny carried his quiet delight
lightly, as if it were just
a job he had to handle, one step
after another, hands steady,
eyes ever steely and alert,
that big glove a Hoover vacuum.
The fans could not see how hard it was,
how hard he tried, how perfectly
he strove to be as flawless
as they wanted him to be.

But his MVP in 64
and all his gloves of gold
were never quite enough to stop
the boos at the rare error,
at those strikeouts at the wrong time.
I was in the stands when they
booed and booed his slumping bat,
until his two late homers
put the Cards, miraculously,
on top.

He was not miraculous
often enough
to be a god of the game, yet
he was a glory under-esteemed,
that almost-greatness that we also need.
So sad to know he died so young.
Superb form must be its own reward.
It never shielded this almost-god
from harm.

Ken Boyer

Lou Brock Running

He seemed to ride golden air,
rocketing just above the ground.
Orbiting the infield, Brock burned
a halo of desire into the day
that seemed to mean the Cards
could only win. After such a run,
after the unimaginable
dream of speed, the bases seemed
to gleam a kind of blessedness.
Nothing much had really changed, and
one run was no more than one run,
but somewhere at the heart of things
Brock's runs to home meant more
than any board of scores could show.

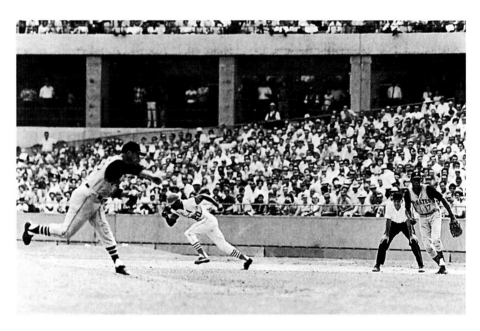

Lou Brock stealing second

Curt Flood in Center

The first game
I saw in the old stadium
(aka Sportsman's Park)
the best
Cardinal center fielder
of all time
just kept on running
under a towering Ernie Banks fly
until all that was left
was the high wall,
which he leapt against,
managing somehow
to hold on to the ball.
Though the wall
knocked him out cold,
he never relaxed his grip.

This is also the story
of how he crashed against
the vast blank wall
of the ball park
we call the Court of Law.
He was the only one
with the timing and the speed
to grasp the real ideal:
a man has rights
of self possession.
Though the wall
knocked him out cold,
he never relaxed his gripe.

The Utility of Mike Shannon

Shannon played any place.
Behind the plate,
in the outfield,
at third base—
he labored in every region,
believing, against all odds,
he could do anything.

A migrant worker
in the field of dreams—
Shannon made hope
into an oddly lovely creed,
but worked his happy faith
with tongue in cheek
and never took himself
too seriously.
Moon Man,
his teammates called him.

Gibson fondly recalls
Shannon at Yankee Stadium
poised with one foot on
the right-field fence,
his glove hand reaching up
as if to pluck
Mantle's towering
homer out of the upper deck.

Gibby queried in disbelief.
Did Shannon think
he could reach that high?
"You never know, big guy.
You never know..."
was Moon Man's reflective reply.

Bob Gibson

A gentle-
man
in his heart of hearts—
he seldom let
his kind side show.

A fierce desire to win
fueled a murderous
ferocity of eye and arm.
Even his catchers
dreaded approaching
his fiery mountain.
"All you know about pitching
is it's hard to hit!"
he snapped at McCarver
more than once.
Off duty he could
play the clown—
sometimes
beating poor Uecker
at his own jokes.

But in his "office"
he was his own personal
real-estate industry—
declaring, again and again,
his ownership
of the corner.

Many a foe
earned a bruised shoulder
by doubting it.

Neither the years
nor the Hall of Fame
has mellowed him.
Don't lean too close
to this poem.

Bob Gibson on the 64 Cardinals

Of all teams I was on, though—
of all the teams I've ever seen—
there was never a better band of men
than the 64 Cardinals.

Bob Gibson

Curt Simmons

Curt had lost his zip when he joined the Cards
but showed in St. Louis what wonders curves,
control, and deft changes of speed could do.
He had an uncanny knack for judging
when he could get away with slow floaters
in the strike zone and when he had to float
them off on wide outside explorations.
Sometimes it was hard to believe the ball
was real, so wide did his wicked ones break.

I saw his famous duel with the great
Aaron, when he duped the homerun king
again and again with a subtle mix
of sudden sharpness and agonizing
slowness until Aaron could stand it no more
and stepped two strides in front of home plate,
whacking the curve before it broke, slamming
it onto the roof in right, only to be
declared out for hitting outside the box.

Elysian Curve

The Arch in St. Louis rainbows up
and round to ground as if it were
what happens to light in light rain
in Manoa, sometimes, day after day.

You can make one, too. Hold a rope
so that the distance between your hands
equals the distance between each hand
and the lowest, dream-warped verve

of the rope's bending down,
and you have made the curve
the Greeks called elysian—
perfect form as a kind of bliss,

like those surprising curves I saw Curt Simmons
bend past Henry Aaron time and time again.
As if the aging hurler cranked
a magic, inner wheel that worked
its charm best against the best.

Ray Sadecki

Being so young and so smart
and so good at what you do,
made you the guy
the bosses picked on again
and again, wanting you
to understand that life
is hard and baseball harder.

You wished you could be
as grizzled and grimacing,
as stern and straining,
as angry and worried
as the other guys,
but your style
must be what it had always been:
smooth and placid,
turmoil held within.

In 64,
winning twenty at
twenty-three years of age,
you were one Bonus Baby
worth every buck,
even if the bosses
found it hard to endure
a kid so young
and so damn cocksure.

Barney Schultz's Ancient Knuckleball
and the Cards' Comeback in 64

To be eleven games back
with thirty-nine games remaining
and to somehow win it all

seems as unlikely
as the arrival of a flying saucer
or of fleeting

superstardom for a rookie
almost ancient enough
to have learned his pitch

from Eddie Cicotte;
seems as unlikely
as a thrown ball

that flutters and weaves—
doing a mambo dance in midair
whose physics seem as uncertain

as the orbit of a moon
(whose seams, somehow,
might not be revolving)

circling a planet
circling, in its turn and turn about,
Alpha Centauri.

Mike Cuellar's Screwball
and the Cards' Comeback in 64

To be eleven games out
with thirty-nine games remaining
made the league crown
seem a place at least
as far away as Las Villas.

Few recountings of that season recall
how often it was Cuellar's recurving curve,
with its unlikely, ingenious
twist of the wrist
at just the right moment,

that made the flight of the ball,
the posture of the batter,
the outcome of the game,
and the history of the season
turn itself inside out.

Catcher

for Tim McCarver

The dove must fly straight to the heart,
the place you have prepared with pain—
your crooked hand swollen that the strike
might live. You kneel for the reliever,
as he frets his small golgotha,
his mound of grief. Eyes pleading with sky,
he's nailed to the cross of his failing
fastball and hanging curve. You lean
before to show the way the ball

must go. Baptist of never ending
perspiration, you must serve up—
again and again and again—
your head upon the plate where
the umpire of all he surveys
may fail once more to save your life,
while all eyes follow the lurid feet,
the batter's prance of twitch and stretch,
leading to what might be the dance
that makes your martyrdom complete.

Bob Uecker

He fielded grounders with a tuba,
won fame for mimicry (some claim
his Harry Caray surpassed the real one),
and fed odd trade rumors (in which he starred)
to gullible reporters. His biggest hits
were comedy routines in which a fool
named Uke (aka Mr. Baseball)
cheerfully suffered deserved pratfalls.

Though deep down he desired the other kind
of fame—the kind that would have made his
legless dad and his many children proud—
at least he proved his first coach wrong, showing
there is a place in baseball for a clown.

In later years his teammates groped for ways
to define the indefinable
magic of Uecker's jests at his own expense,
the jokes that were so much more than funny.

McCarver remembers best the clubhouse scene,
after the Cards had finished off the Yanks.
Uke, who rode the bench all seven games,
was barefoot dancing an exquisite
broken-glass gavotte, spinning and leaping,
in the midst of the victory-maddened moment,
risking life and limb for the year's last laugh.

Bob Uecker on How to Catch
Barney Schultz's Knuckleball

Wait for the ball
to stop rolling,
then pick it up.

Johnny Keane, Manager

His name fit his finely sharpened mind,
but kindness and patience were what
his teams remembered most. He could be hard
when he had to be, and confronted Groat
on the matter of the hit and run.

As always, Johnny worked it out;
accord remained his one religion
of field, dugout, clubhouse, hotel, and bar.
A saintly man in a barbarous job,
he swore by his belief in Cardinals.

Gibson found heightened grace in the light
of Keane's confidence and made believers
of every man that dared to raise a bat
against the dream of winning all the way
through to where there would be no more to prove.

Keane's name also implies lamentation,
and he had sorrows on the field and off,
but, after two decades of the bush leagues,
he had his two months of unexpected joy.
An impossibility became fact.
The next year's failure could not undo that.

The Tragic Fall of the Phillies in 64

Some failures are sublime—grand
views from the loftiest of heights
followed by, necessarily,
precipitous, echoing dives
into vast canyons of lost hype.

Oedipus, driven to root out
the evil nesting in the heart
of his almost magnificence,
was destroyed by a sudden, tidal
resurge of terrible knowledge.

Gene Mauch, endeavoring to make
assurance double sure, vowed
he'd pitch his favorite aces,
Bunning and Short, on two days rest
until they'd clinched the pennant.

Let us be silent a moment.

The Miracle at Grand and Dodier

The miracle at Coogan's Bluff,
climaxed with
the shot heard round
the New York newspapers.

The 1951 Giants had come back
miraculously
after being 13½ games out
with 44 games remaining.

Thomas Kiernan,
in his 1975 book declared
the Giant's comeback unique,
saying "there had been nothing
close to it in the eighty year
history of major-league baseball."

It could be
Kiernan was right
concerning
the eighty years
that came before 1951,
if that is what he meant.

But thirteen years after 1951
and eleven years before 1975
the Cardinals came back
miraculously
after being 11 games back
with 39 games remaining.

The country of baseball
is large
with room for many miracles.

Lonborg and Champagne

There are many annoyances in Ken Burns'
paean to the National Pastime,
but his blinkered obsessions with New York
and Boston teams seem his cardinal sins.

One of the most striking absurdities:
the lugubrious lament over Boston's
failure to go all the way in 67—
a tear-jerking tale that fails to understand

how much of the real rest of America
was very happy about that turn of events,
which seemed so fitting in the face
of outrageous Red Sox arrogances

that so delightfully
spurred the Cardinals on.

The Dream of Being Carl Warwick

To be Gibson or Groat, Boyer or Brock was beyond belief. The stars who light up the sky night after night, soar entirely celestial and out of our reach—bright lights to wish upon, but not guys we could aspire to be.

But to be Carl Warwick—to be the unknown guy whose World Series claim to fame was his somehow slapping three pinch hits in a row—hits without which two games and the series might not have been won—seemed somehow possible. Deep in my myth of myself lurked the implausible suspicion that, given the chance, I could step out of my shadow to win the prize with a sweet and timely swat or two or three.

The dream begins, oddly enough, in Sophomore English class where I am belaboring my essay about a character in Thornton Wilder's *Our Town*. I am putting the finishing touches on my unlikely account of the tragic World War I demise of Joe Crowell, crippled newspaper boy of Grover's Corners. I am attempting to wield what I imagine to be Hemingwayesque prose to give this good Joe a suitably horrible big finish in a greenish haze of poison gas, when I hear the sound of spikes echoing down the corridors of Ritenour Senior High School.

Suddenly the classroom door jerks open, and the wizened face of Johnny Keane, in cap and full uniform, leans in. He aims a determined glower at my teacher, Miss Borgelt, and barks out, "I've come for Carl Warwick. We're going to need him today."

Miss Borgelt begins to explain that there are no Carls in this class and declares, "There must be some mistake...."

But Keane is already in our midst. Hulking impatiently over me as I write of Joe Crowell's last gasp for breath, writhing in agony. "There you are Warwick," Keane almost shouts as he yanks me vertically from my desk, "Let's get going. We need to reach the stadium by three p.m. You heard me, Warwick, let's get going."

And I find myself strapped into the back seat of some absurdly scarlet Anheuser-Busch company car and hurtling down the highway toward the stadium. "Yeah, yeah, that's what they all say," is all Keene replies each time I try to tell him who I really am. He later explains that every major league team has a nonexistent player on its roster for just these sorts of occasions. He mentions this bizarre policy in a casual, peremptory way, as if to say, "Any idiot would understand this is how it has to be."

Before I know it I am out on the early evening field fully uniformed. On my back is the number 17 and W A R W I C K spelled out in large letters. I later learn that all nonexistent players are given the numbers 16 or 17. It is a code that all the teams accept.

In some patches this dream seems too flattering sweet to be substantial, as I find myself mingling with my gods to take batting practice on the field of illumined green. The familiar vague roar of the crowd seems somehow severe and menacing from the vantage of the field, the rolling thunder of a storm I fear will break me in half.

Meanwhile, an insincerely solicitous Bob Uecker is keeping up a steady banter of annoying remarks along the lines of "Eh, *Warwick*, you're lookin' a bit short today! Ha, ha, ha!" and "Heh, *Warwick*, you'd better tie yourself down, here comes a breeze!" With grim determination I keep reminding myself that Keane must have chosen me for a reason...

This is one of those dreams whose descents never hit bottom. I always wake before I come to bat. But in another dream I find myself Warwick again. This time it is many years after 1964 and I discover myself inexplicably in conversation with Mickey Mantle at a banquet of some sort. As baseball heroes of the same era, we are seated together, and Mantle is trying to understand who the heck I am. "Ah," says The Mick at last, "so you were their number 17... We used our number 16 for pitching and that time our Whitey Ford just didn't quite have the stuff..."

Dal Maxvill Catches the
Last Pop Fly of 1964

It had been a year of grief and fear
and so many sorts of uncertainty—
the sixties were erupting
all over America,
all over the world.
The season had been

bizarre,
like nothing anyone
could have imagined,
but here it was:
Bobby Richardson,
jammed by a Gibson fastball,

high and tight,
popping it up to right
and Maxvill settling under it
with Dick Groat shouting—
"Don't let it hit you in the coconut, Max"—
while it fell and fell

through the chilled air
fibrous with fragments of October's lost leaves,
through several centuries of clouds,
while birds wheeled and wheeled
finding altitude for long flights,
while an unseen airplane buzzed somewhere

off on the margins of someone's life,
and thirty-three thousand souls
packed into Busch Stadium
held their breaths
till there came
the POP in the glove,

then the shouting that seemed
as if it would go on for years,
a tumult everyone could see arriving
with a surety like few things in this world
because Maxvill had sure hands;
everyone knew Maxvill had sure hands.

Sure hands.

Tim McCarver, Ken Boyer and Bob Gibson celebrate after the last out of the 1964 World Series

The Accidental Joe Hoerner

His pitching was as accident free
as it could be. His tiny ERAs
made him the perfect short relief.

But off the mound he was purest collision.
His teenaged auto wreck almost did him in
and forced a change in his pitching motion.

And then there were his feats as a Cardinal.
His bumper-carring the team bus to the hotel
when the driver failed to show up on time.

Or the bottle of Boston post–Series champagne
that exploded spectacularly in his hands,
shards of glass cutting fingers and tendons.

Or the time he fired a fastball up up and away
at the window of the stadium club in L.A.,
finding out, too late, the glass could be broken.

Roger Maris, Redbird

When Roger Maris played for the Cards,
he was an extraordinary star,
helping the Birds to a pair of pennants.
But he wasn't the Roger of yore,
the bomber of 61 or 64.

In 65 the Yanks had kept him on the field,
not telling him of broken bone
that should have been allowed to heal.
So when he came to the Cards in 67
his left-hand power grip was lost to him,

and home runs had become unlikely,
but he had taught himself to hit with
a largely backhand stroke, letting his
strong right arm guide the bat to spray
singles here and there, bunting often,

calculating always how to move
the runners along or bring them home.
St. Louis fans loved his hustle;
his stellar play on the field;
his selfless, timely hitting.

Yankee fan Robert Wuhl
claims Maris was better loved
in his first at bat at Busch
than he had ever been
in five seasons in New York.

Roger Eugene Maris and William Cullen Bryant

"Whither ... dost thou pursue thy solitary way?"
—William Cullen Bryant, "To a Waterfowl"

Maris smacked 61 in 61,
but number 58's the one
that Kubek likes to recollect:

Roger, backing out of the box
to watch a flock of two-hundred
high-honking geese shape their classic V
right above the overhang in right
at old Tiger Stadium;

Roger, at rest in the peaceful eye
of his fierce, cyclonic year,
calmly considering the clouds
until the last bird had flapped past,
while thousands watched his watching;

Roger, stepping back in and whacking
the very next pitch four hundred feet,
high into the upper deck, just below
where he'd seen the geese go—
a guided, a certain flight, Bryant
would say, despite the boundless sky.

Ford Frick's Asterisk

Asterisk means "a little star,"
and for a time a tiny light
belittled the record 61
that Maris socked in 61.

Sure, Roger had more games than Ruth,
but his season lacked the absurdly
easy right-field fence that Babe
enjoyed at every chance he got

to maul the mediocre pitching
St. Louie Brownies at Sportsman's Park
in 27, the year he notched his 60.
The Browns wisely screened off

that easy pop in 29.
Maybe Frick should have asterisked
the Ruth record, too: every
little star should have its shine.

Al Hrabosky, "The Mad Hungarian"

This passionate pitcher—
handsome, hirsute, darkly glowering,
Fu-Manchu-mustachioed—
would stalk off the mound,
turn his back to the hitter,
and listen intently for moments
that stretched out like weeks
to whatever demons were speaking to him
from the empty centerfield seats.

And then, signaling his readiness
by pounding ball into glove, he would whirl
and turn the gathered horror of his angered gaze
toward the poor sap at the plate,
who was waiting—nervously, nervously—
armed only with a stick of wood.

And then, at last, the long-awaited pitch:
a laser beam dead-on to the target
propelled as much by attitude as by arm speed.

During his two best years with the Cards,
the fans adored his Rasputin-esque routine.
When Alston snubbed him for the All-Star team,
the fans turned a game against the Dodgers
into a "We Hlove Hrabosky" banner day
and the Mad Hungarian got the win,
amid hloving hbanners sporting jibes like
"The Smog Is Not the Densest Thing in L.A."

THE 1980S AND 90S

White Rat in a Maze

amazing what intelligence can do
against obstacle after obstacle
when they score one, you score two

finding a way around each corner
when they score three, you score four
by speed or pitching or fielding

or the canny trade or refusal to trade
of one star for another or having
the luck or the genius to bring up
that reed-thin rookie reliever
at just the right time to win
and win and win again beyond

what would seem to be logic
but somehow making it make sense
to the bafflement of all whose

jobs depend on the impossibility
of staying ahead of your strange
singles-tapping teams that win and win

The Wizard of Oz

As we danced up the yellow-striped ramp,
glimpsing in every gap
a world bizarrely green,
we knew who we were off to see:

a man with magic grasp of any trick
of ball by bat or bounce,
in glove or hand,
pulling wins out of his hat,

helping the Cards possess the heart,
the brains, the courage;
clicking his ruby spikes,
because there's no place like home

to score and score for a town
that needed to believe,
above and beyond absurd
Clydesdales of a different color,

that even a little guy can fly,
maybe, if desire wings,
ballooning beyond Kansas,
somersaulting fields of dream.

Glenn Brummer, Third-String Catcher and Possibly the Slowest Runner in the National League, Steals Home to Help the Cardinals Win the 1982 Pennant

In the bottom
of the twelfth,
while strolling

further and further and further and further
off third,
heavy-hoofed Glenn Brummer

suddenly realizes
the Giants are entirely
oblivious.

Willie McGee Almost Singlehandedly Wins
Game Three of the 1982 World Series

The New York writers called him ET
because he seemed shy and otherwordly
and because his ears stuck out
like the endearing alien's in the movie,

and in game three in Milwaukee
the homers he hit
and the homers he took away
by his uncanny catches in center
exceeded earthly understanding.

He deserved an X-file all his own,
as he became an unidentified flying outfielder,
snatching the extraterrestrial ball
high above the wall.

Herzog said if Willie'd
done this in New York it'd be
called the greatest performance ever.
Still, a few writers knew
it was time to phone home.

The truth was out there.

Sutter's Sinker from Hell

Some hurled balls can overturn worlds.
Candy Cummings' bedazzling curve,
invented for the Hartford Dark Blues
somewhere around 1872
baffled batters then and ever since;
likewise Whitlow Wyatt's sneaky slider,
contrived for the 40s Dodgers.

And then Fred Martin engineered
the split-fingered fastball, and taught
it to his first and best pupil,
a guy Whitey Herzog would come
to call "a bullpen named Bruce."

Sutter's "sinker from hell"
made him as close to perfect
as any pitcher can get:
in the playoffs in 82
his ERA stood at
a well-rounded 0.00.

The secret, Sutter said, was speed.
The batters had no way to tell
his straight 86 m.p.h. heaters
from his 82 m.p.h. splitters.

So the gentle, bushy-bearded Bruce—
who loved to go fishing for days,
hardly moving, adrift in vast lakes—
became the guru of the ideal,
the almost unhittable pitch;
became the most feared of hurlers,
who could make the strongest men weep,
as they found themselves swinging,
with chagrined disbelief, at balls
already dead and buried at their feet.

Joaquin Andujar

To describe himself Joaquin
favored the phrase "one tough Dominican,"
and he could be rough on hitters,
winning game after game
when he was feeling fine.

In the series in 82
Ted Simmons bounced one off his leg
and poor Andujar was carried away.
He writhed in agony for hours
and hobbled around on crutches for days.

But then
a suddenly cured Joaquin
pitched the Series final
and won.

John Tudor's Control

Control smartly employed can warm
a box score more than radar-seeking heat.
That's why a Maddux or a Tudor
can win game after game, day after day,
with only a modest sprinkling of Ks.

Hit 'em where their bats ain't
and at an angle or a speed
they are not fully primed to time,
staying ahead on the count,
keeping the hitter off stride.

Quiet John's precision was premised on
the guys behind him—their dazzling defense,
their speed, their surprising, timely offense.
When Tudor pitched there often turned out to be,
miraculously, just enough runs to win.

Although he lacked the passion of Andujar,
John could elegantly cool the batters.
Tudor was Ingres to Andujar's Delacroix,
and both could be masters of their pieces.

The Tarpaulin and the Hare

In the playoffs in 85
Vince Coleman, the Card's speed demon,
was famously overtaken
by the painstakingly slow rolling
of Busch stadium's tarpaulin.

But slow and steady wins the race
is not the moral in this case.
The truth Coleman should have foreseen:
don't turn your back on a machine.

Jack Gets a Whack Heard Round Some Worlds

Herzog had a deck of Cards that let him
pull fast ones, stacking dinky singles,
swiped bases, uncanny fielding, stingy pitching—
all the little numbers that can still, somehow,

add up to beating the flashier sharpers,
but Herzog often had at least
one fancy face card up his sleeve—
a Jack of Clark who could slug 'em hard and far.

Jack had always dreamed
of winning it all with just one blow,
as Bobby Thomson did in 51,
but the Bums Jack faced

in the playoffs in 85 mostly walked him
when there were any men on base,
until that fateful moment
top of the ninth, two out and two on,

the final game of the playoffs,
the Dodgers ahead 5 to 4.
With one swing Jack changed that to 7–5,
and the Redbird's October was still alive.

The Cardinals Win the 1985 World Series

In every video replay of the game
till the end of time
Todd Worrell's foot slaps first
and the Cards win the Series
they lost the next day.

The St. Louis Cardinals in Aiea in 1997: On the Occasion When My Team, After My Twenty-five-year Absence from Their Town, Came to Me

In the ninth,
with the Cards ahead by one
and Eckersley
islanded on the mound,

three egrets lifted off—
one,   two,   three,
great wings of white
above the grandstand—

as sweetly
as those last three outs
counted down
in just the right way.

A sunset was rising, too,
as the momentary hush
readied a
roar.

Fernando Tatis Hits Two
Grand Slams in One Inning

They were the first
he'd ever hit.
What are the odds?
Two swings: eight runs.

Maybe this means
anything can happen:
world peace,
an end to hunger,

the merciful
cancellation
of every sitcom on TV,
a cure for all disease.

The Tatis miracle
brings despair,
however briefly,
to its knees.

McGwire's Greatest Swing Came After

And it was not with his bat.
It came when he crossed the plate
and swung little Matt McGwire

high in the air,
showing he loved his son
more than his 62nd homerun.

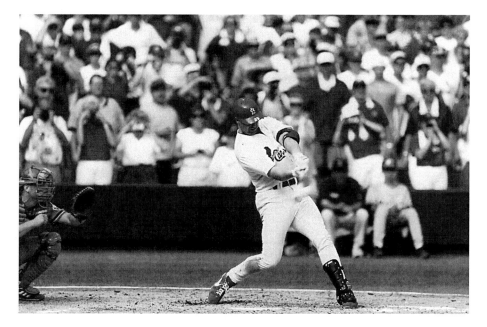

Mark McGwire slugs homer number 70 in 1998 (photograph by Brian Spurlock)

Mark and Sammy Versus Leo the Lip

When McGwire and Sosa
cranked their tallies
into the sixties,
while saying all those admiring
things about each other,

it reminded us how grand
this game could be,
how nice guys could finish
first and second.
It seemed to speak

of ancient days,
when Alex Cartwright
and company could play
mostly
for camaraderie.

Committing Harry Caray in the Windy City

For the record
and to correct the remembrances
of a Cardinal point of my childhood,
it has to be said.

The Cubs own,
till the end of time,
the mad,
passionate heart
of that ultimate
prima-donna,
coarse-voiced crooner
of the baseball microphone.

Profile shots
of every single one
of Slammin' Sammy's
stadium-long swings
in 98
showed him wearing
Harry Caray on his sleeve
for TVs
and front pages
all over America
to see.

The least camera-ready
radio broadcaster in world history
had his face in our face
for more than half a year,
keeping him out
in that old ball game.

But it's his voice,
so ingrained
irretrievably
in the heartwood of our minds,
that makes us care, so deeply,
that he'll never come back.

On Trying to Write a Mark McGwire

If I could hit off seventy baseball
poems that go beyond my walls, that fly
beyond what stops me short of my home plate

for more at bats than I'd care to admit.
If I could do it, I'd set the record;
I'd have the first ever all–Cardinal,

book-length sequence that's fit for print.
Like Mark McGwire, I try to be a modest guy.
I'd not claim a surge past Tom Clark's

fine hitting for his Pirate picture book.
I'd not say that my seventy biggest whacks
flew past the Bronx-bombing, Ruth-full high signs

of Rodney Torreson's ripened pinstripes,
even though I've often wished his Yankees,
the bullies of a brutal town, were damned.

My sequence badgers me with constant questions.
Some nick my corners. Some sail outside.
Some are high and tight. Some are inside and low.

Every time out—both before and after—
the same question wears its many words:
Will I? Can I? I try to be polite.

I listen carefully. I talk it out,
even though I am the only one asking,
even though I am the only one listening,

even though all the interviews are only
my head talking and talking to my head,
even though all this is only verse,

or adverse, a striking at the pitch
of thought curving to the spin of syntax.
The questions come when I hit several

stanzas right away, or when I strike out
looking for the perfect slant of word.
I'll need at least sixty to fill the covers,

for a first ever record-breaking collection.
I've got more than thirty and I'll keep
on swinging. Will my streak hold steady?

THE 2000S

Will Clark's Last Aria

Only a Redbird for a mere two months
in the extraordinary summer
of the first year of the new millennium—
Will managed to be amazingly on key.

Finding himself discarded by the orange birds
(that once were, in St. Louis, brown),
his bat sparked bright trills, *con fuoco*,
from the first day he switched his cap to red,

and he rose as few performers ever do
to the music's sternest occasions
where one precise right note can win the song.
After this unexpected masterseason,

he did what even fewer performers do,
retiring with a flourish, a crescendo.

Dreaming with the Great Rookie, Albert Pujols

As the summer of 2001 draws to a close,
Albert Pujols seems manna from heaven.
A fearless, extraordinary young man—
equally at home in infield and outfield
who hits for power and for average—
he's a kid that doesn't act his age.
As they said about Musial his first year,
"How can anybody be this good?"
Dreaming grandeur for a just-begun career
can be a risky game, but it is what
we should do, what we need to do.

As with the butterfly and Chuang Tzu,
what might turn out to be true is real, too.

September 17, 2001

There were flags everywhere
when baseball came back on air
seven days after the horror
and there were moving prayers
for all the terribly murdered.

At every stadium there were
salutes to troops of police and fire
and other workers of rescue.
There were songs and placards
and chants of U-S-A, U-S-A.

And in St. Louis there was
the venerable Jack Buck,
our lost Harry's better half,
trembling with his dis-ease
but with a voice still rich and clear,

reading for us his rhymed reasons.

Game Called, 2002

after Grantland Rice and for Darryl Kile

Game called by darkness—let the curtain fall.
No more the sharp, inclining curveball bends.

One who taught the spheres how to descend
no more makes shapely throws to earn the call.

DK has left us with the night to face,
and there is no one who can take his place.

A life just started, with so many starts to go.
Game called—a silence settles on Chicago.

Stealing Home, 2001

arriving in a strange city
    ideally the play is tried with two outs
where I was once a child
    and less than two strikes on the batter
I meet the first crocuses of spring
    left-handers using full wind-ups
fierce salvos of color fired through
    provide the best chance
pale ironies of melting snow
    you will need about four seconds
as I imagine the flowers unfolding
    to cover the distance
faces from childhood
    from leadoff to headlong slide
come unexpectedly to mind

POSTGAME POINTS

Legends of the Old Ballgame

"...we think of them as 'just anecdotes' that happened to no one in particular."
—Tristram Coffin, "The Folklore of Baseball"

Could it all be merely legend after all?

Maybe a particular rookie never wired home from
    spring training, "Put another cup of water in
    the soup, Ma, they started throwing curves
    today."

Maybe no batter we can name struck out on three
    called strikes while staring at a new-fangled
    airplane buzzing overhead.

Maybe no real slugger ever told a sick kid he'd hit a
    homer for him, and then went and did it.

Maybe there was never a pitcher so fast he could snag
    a strikeout by faking three pitches while the
    catcher walloped his mitt three times.

Maybe a home run king never called a flag pole shot.
    Maybe the actual air was fingered only to
    declare, "Hey! I've got one more strike, you
    bastards!"

Maybe a brash Gas House Gang fireballer never warned
    the Dodgers he'd throw them all fastballs all
    day, then shut them out.

Maybe a huge, affable, Paul Bunyan–like figure never
    came out of the far West to became the toast of
    a Midwestern city, while hitting 70 huge
    home runs.

Such things are unlikely in fact.
In fact, maybe the game itself does not exist and
    hovers only as a rumor of stadiums over blighted
    urban vacancies of the heart.

A Brief History of the Baseball Movie

Joe E. roars his Model T straight through
the right field wall to reach the mound to pitch
silly lies that ring true to Lardner's tale.
To win a world serious is where
it must somehow contrive to end.

But, whatever the score, it always starts again,
happening every spring where hope hops
eternal for Ray Milland, juicing his balls
to win big games for the St. Louis team
and get the girl and tenure at Wash U, too.

Gary Cooper's acting gets its whacks,
despite his not knowing how to hold a bat,
but Gehrig died so young this sweetly painful
paean to Yankee pride could co-star the Babe
himself, whose classic swings are fine to see.

Dutch Reagan, future president, wins one
for the country by striking out those damn Yankees,
and Dan Dailey, as Dizzy Dean, does in
the Tigers and the English language—
all for the public good, the movie decrees.

Sometimes biopic truth shifts its trajectory,
as when courageous Jimmy Piersal steps
upward toward the light to conclude the film—
Tony Perkins flicking here a double-play
relay to Freud and barely surviving
fatherly fields of well-meant demeaning,

but in other plots our fathers must play
their games of catch with us across their deaths,
where, if we dream we build it, they return
to Kinsella's or Costner's or any other
lost little leaguer's private Iowa.

But it's only natural, as Redford shows,
smacking it far beyond the failure
unmerciful Malamud makes his Hobbs.

Indeed, we need that last majestic blast,
that homer that breaks up the sky.
It's baseball's necessary cliché,
an ending so exquisitely emphatic
we don't care that it always comes back,

banging its drum slowly to recollect
that, even in these Edenic, summer greens,
we can sail out like final flights of balls
into cloudy heights turned celluloid,
circling and recircling, round and round
our childhoods' forgotten myths of home.

Bugs Bunny Traded to the Cardinals
for a Duck Dodger to Be Named Later

In *Baseball Bugs* Warner Brothers
has the inimitable rabbit
play every position on the field,
and several off, to defeat
the haplessly thuggish
Gas House Gorillas.

Despite the Brooklyn accent
Mel Blanc's voice lends
to the greatest cartoon character
ever to play Major League Baseball,
the analogy does not hold.

Bugs would have had to be with the Cards
rather than with those Brooklyn Bums.
Except for all the things
he does with his long ears,
Bug's manic style of play
is Pepper Martin all the way.

Double-play Duos

Great hands and feet at second and short
can give a team the sweetest piece of mind.
Knowing a Groat and Javier, a Smith and Herr,
a Marion and Schoendienst wait to bind

the wound that is the middle of the field,
to make one-on and one-out into an end
of what might have been a rally,
helps the pitcher fire his fast one and bend

his curve, helps all fielders hone their play
in hopes of that most graceful solution
where move and counter move become ballet,
a dance under the lights or in the sun—

finding in a choreography of fear
the celestial music of a sphere.

A Collection of Cardinal Pitches

1. Dizzy Dean's Fastball

   The briefest distance
   between
   two hands.

   A moon
   that shrinks
   to a microbe.

2. Bruce Sutter's Split-Finger Fastball

   A pitch
   that seems

   to come
   too quick

   to fall
   so far.

3. Curt Simmons' Curve

   A tail
   that wags
   the batter.

   A fruit
   that picks
   itself.

   A revolving door
   to the minor
   leagues.

4. Bob Gibson's Slider

   Anger
   dreaming.

   A sinister
   sidespin twirl

   breaking
   at the last minute

   the batter's
   heart.

5. Harry Brecheen's Screwball

   His curveball's
   evil twin.

   An ampersand
   in air.

6. Jesse Haines' Knuckleball

   An earthquake
   on the wing.

   A dance
   to no tune
   at all.

   A pigeon
   changing
   its mind.

7. Burleigh Grimes' Spitball

   Startlingly
   curvacious.

   A breaking ball,
   tawdry and overdressed,

   twirling its pearls.

8. Mort Cooper's Brushback

   Assassination's
   kissing cousin.

   A little skull
   with a big
   grin.

The Sorrow of the Big Trade

How could the Cardinals have traded
White and Boyer? Flood and McCarver?
When such a trade's in hand and in the news
it's hard for fans to come to understand.
Yea, it's just part of the business,
part of the game. That's what the owners say.
And, of course, it is true. Teams are made
as well as lost that way. The Cardinals
of 64 would not have come to pass

without the fortunate pilfering
of Brock from Chicago, Groat from Pittsburgh.
Even a seeming absurd misfortune can turn out
to be a good thing—the trading of Hornsby
for Frankie Frisch seemed to fans insane,
but as the seasons changed Frisch proved to be
a gain, a benefit well worth the price.
We all know that such deals are in the cards,
but as they come and go, to and from the Cards,

there is a sense of loss that goes beyond
the rational. We try to remember
that these people belong to themselves only
and must make their own way in a world
that visits all of us, player and fan alike,
with larger misfortunes than changes of city.
And yet the sorrow and the anger come—
small lessons in the commerce of grief
and the stock exchange of pity.

Autumnal Fields of Almost

"It breaks your heart. It is designed to break your heart."
—A. Bartlett Giamatti, "Green Fields of the Mind"

Giamatti's lament for Boston
speaks to the core of every fan's regret.

Rooters for those who do not, at last, win—
but should have or could have or might have won,

if only this or that or the other
had happened or not happened or or or...

(the what-ifs never end)—taste the bitter-
sweet of baseball as winning fans do not.

Phillies fans in the fall of 64
or Cards fans in the first fall of the new

millennium feel the pain for which
"wait till next year" is not much of a cure.

Each hope must keep its counterweight in view.
Expected sorrows teach us to endure.

Index of Titles and First Lines

Index of People